Dear Smarty-pants,

This book reminds me of us: it's a combination of your penchant for random tales driven by an insatiable curiosity, + my ability provide them humourously while making no sense whatsoever.

Practise up, because I intend to gather a <u>LOT</u> of stories in L.A., which I will recount to you in riddle form.

Au revoir, ma chère Rebecca. I will miss your witty company immensely!

You are kindred.

Love,

Allie

WHAT'S THE STORY?

by Matthew Johnstone

foreword by Dr. Edward de Bono

design by Annie Schwebel

Stewart, Tabori & Chang

New York

For my family and friends.
—Matthew Johnstone

Published in 1999 by
Stewart, Tabori & Chang
A division of U.S. Media Holdings, Inc.
115 West 18th Street
New York, NY 10011

Distributed in Canada by
General Publishing Company Ltd.
30 Lesmill Road
Don Mills, Ontario, Canada M3B 2T6

Library of Congress Cataloging-in-Publication Data
Johnstone, Matthew.
    What's the story? / by Matthew Johnstone : foreword by
Edward De Bono.
        p.   cm.
    ISBN 1-55670-886-6 (alk. paper)
    1. Puzzles.   2. Lateral thinking.   I. Title
    GV1507.L37J65   1999   98-43780
    793.73—dc21   CIP

Printed in Hong Kong
10 9 8 7 6 5 4 3 2 1
First Printing

FOREWORD

For 2400 years, we have allowed the Greek Gang of Three (Socrates, Plato, and Aristotle) to convince us that thinking was all about logic. This is the equivalent of saying that a motor car is all about the front left wheel. The front left wheel is both essential and excellent—but not enough by itself.

We now know that most of the errors of thinking are errors of perception. Yet logic does not touch perceptions; logic only plays around with the pieces produced by perception. That is why there was a need for "Lateral Thinking," which I described in my 1967 book *New Think*. Just as the Theory of Relativity had been in action for millions of years before Einstein, in describing it, gave it form and definition, my role was to describe lateral thinking and to show its importance.

Creativity is not just a matter of messing around and hoping an idea will emerge. You cannot dig a hole in a different place by digging the same hole deeper. Trying harder with the same approach will not work. Trying harder with the same concepts and perceptions may also not work. Hence the need to "change" approaches, concepts, and perceptions.

That is precisely what this book is about. It is an excellent collection of such lateral thinking stimulants, all of them beautifully illustrated.

Try them. Think about them. Discuss them with your friends. Watch your thinking as you tackle them. In this way you can build up the attitude of lateral thinking.

You can analyze the past—but you have to design the future.

EDWARD DE BONO

www.edwdebono.com

RULES OF PLAY

Having a somewhat dark sense of humor, Lateral Thinking Puzzles—with their recurring themes of bizarre deaths, circus oddities, other people's misfortunes, and just outright stupid situations—have always appealed to me. Lateral Thinking Puzzles are really like matured riddles. The beauty of these bitter and twisted tales lies in how you solve them. You can try to figure out these stories on your own, but just remember that no one will be around to marvel at your brilliance or offer congratulatory slaps on the back. So it's my recommendation that you play with two or more people—the more, the better. The rules are very straightforward.

1. Choose the "Knowing One." This person is the storyteller and, unlike the rest of the group, knows the solution to the story in advance (by referring to the answers in the back). In a group, players can take turns being the Knowing One.

2. The Knowing One reads the story to the eager gathering of "Inquisitors." The Inquisitors are able to ask questions to which the Knowing One (who, at times, will be bursting to say more) may only reply "Yes," "No," or "Irrelevant."

3. Each story comes with its very own picture. No doubt, you will scrutinize it for clues—but there are very few and these will probably only become evident after the story has been solved. The pictures serve to entertain your eyeballs when your mind goes blank.

There is no real point or moral to any of these stories, except to expand your mind, test your powers of deduction, improve the way you may question any situation, make you realize how many assumptions you make, and, above all, break up boring car trips and save otherwise dull dinner parties. I hope you get as much pleasure from solving these stories as I did from drawing them. Good luck and have fun.

Matthew Johnstone

Three well-dressed women stand huddled together. The

One who is crying has never been happier and the

Two who are smiling have never been more miserable.

What is going on

?

A MAN WAKES UP FROM A DRUNKEN STUPOR.

HE TURNS ON THE LIGHT,

ST^U M BLES   TO THE WINDOW,

LOOKS   O U T

THEN HANGS HIMSELF.

WHY?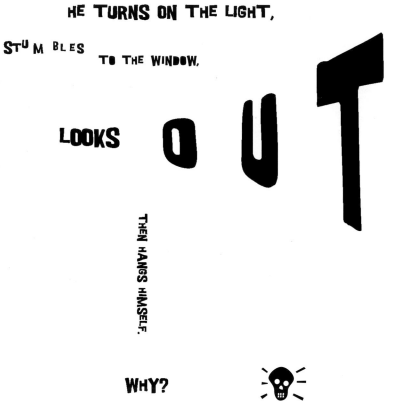

An anthropologist
    discovers
  a perfect body frozen in
a glacier
    and exclaims...

"THIS IS
ADAM!"

How does he know?

What do you think? it looks pretty good" "I wouldn't touch it. Come on it's ripe for the picking. what can possibly go wrong. I just have a really bad feeling about this Adam." "oh come on you have a bad feeling about everything Eve, you're such a worrier" "don't give me that macho crap, go ahead eat it BUT don't say I didn't warn you "Oh so now this becomes a little questions. Oh stop it, you're such a control freak just look what we've got here. I can't believe you're prepared to jeopardize it. this. Fine, ahead you'll be back .... — Eve your snake pal here.
CRUNCH!!

A man rEquired stitches and banDagiNG After an excited coNveRSatioN in a Phone booth.

WhY?

While working in a western
country, a Chinese

performer decides to defect.
He makes a hasty escape
on his bicycle and rides
until he can ride no more.
He falls asleep on the side
of the road, where he
is discovered three months
later, still sound asleep.

How can this be?

A woman jumps off

a 44 storey building.

As she sails past the

22nd floor she hears

a phone ringing and

instantly regrets her

decision. why?

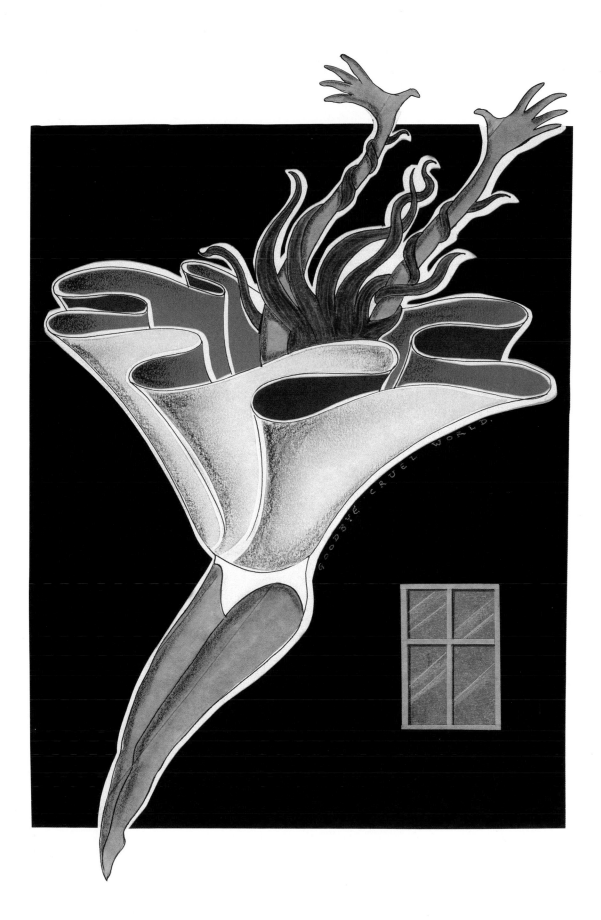

Five men meander along a
path. It starts to rain and
four of them dash for cover.

The fifth makes no attempt
to move any faster yet arrives
at the same time still looking
dapper and totally dry.

How?

a man

sticks his hand up
a woman's dress

and what f o l l o w s

is much
m
m
a
y
h
e
m,

VIOLENCE,
VIOLENCE,
and hilarity.

What's going on?

THE PRESIDENT PULLS INTO A SMALL TOWN DECIDING IT IS TIME FOR A HAIR CUT. THERE ARE ONLY TWO BARBERS TO CHOOSE FROM.

ONE HAS AN ATROCIOUS HAIRCUT AND MESSY SHOP. THE OTHER, A SNAPPY HAIRCUT AND A CLEAN SHOP.

THE PRESIDENT OPTS FOR THE MESSY BARBER. WHY?

A father and son are involved in a car accident. The father is killed instantly and the son is rushed to hospital. The surgeon enters the operating ROOM and says "I can not operate on this boy. He is my Son!"

HOW can this be?

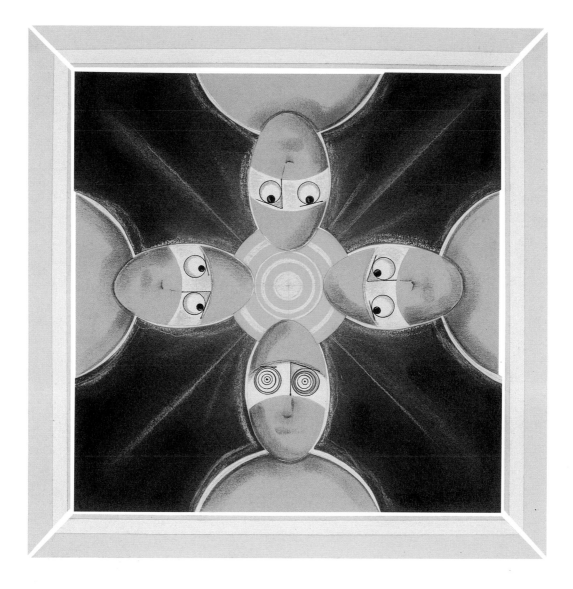

gift

···· a man gives a woman a **bottomless** to place ¶

flesh, blood, and bone into.¶

She is *delighted!*

What is it?¶

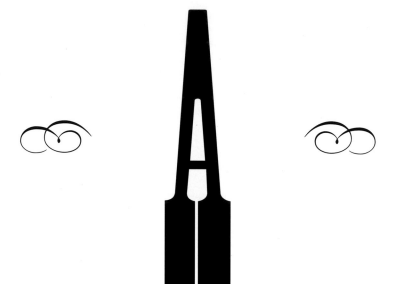

WOMAN TAKES HER HUSBAND TO A WESTERN.
DURING THE FINAL SHOWDOWN, SHE PULLS
OUT A PISTOL, SHOOTS HIM, THEN CASUALLY
REMOVES THE BODY FROM THE THEATER
WITHOUT ANYONE BEING THE WISER. HOW?

The normally generous
man was totally unenamored
by the deaf, mute boy's

plea for charity. Why?

a woman and man are driving
through a rough part of town when
they run out of gas.
The man tells the woman to stay
in the car, keep the doors locked,
and the windows shut

He returns with gasoline to find
his wife unconscious and a stranger

in the car.

what happened?

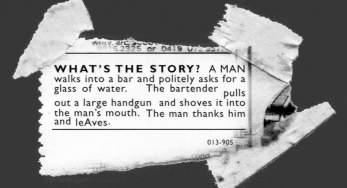

WHAT'S THE STORY? A MAN
walks into a bar and politely asks for a
glass of water.   The bartender pulls
out a large handgun and shoves it into
the man's mouth. The man thanks him
and leAves.

013-90S

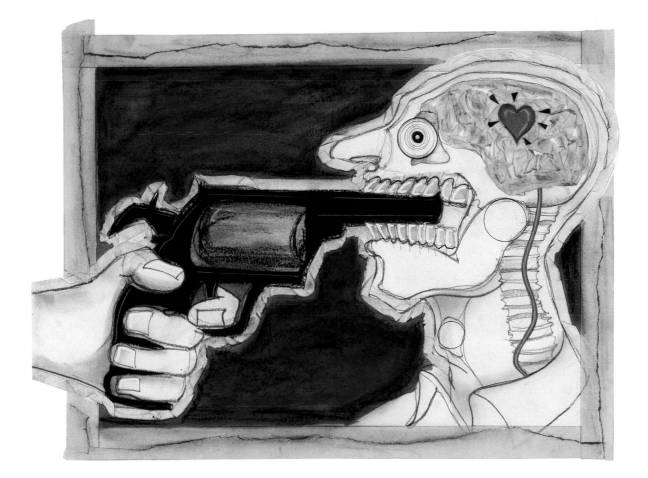

⊕

THE ORGAN STOPPED

⊕

THE CONGREGATION

FELL SILENT AS THE

ROBED MAN PLUNGED

TO HIS DEATH.

HE WAS MURDERED.

⊕

HOW?

⊕

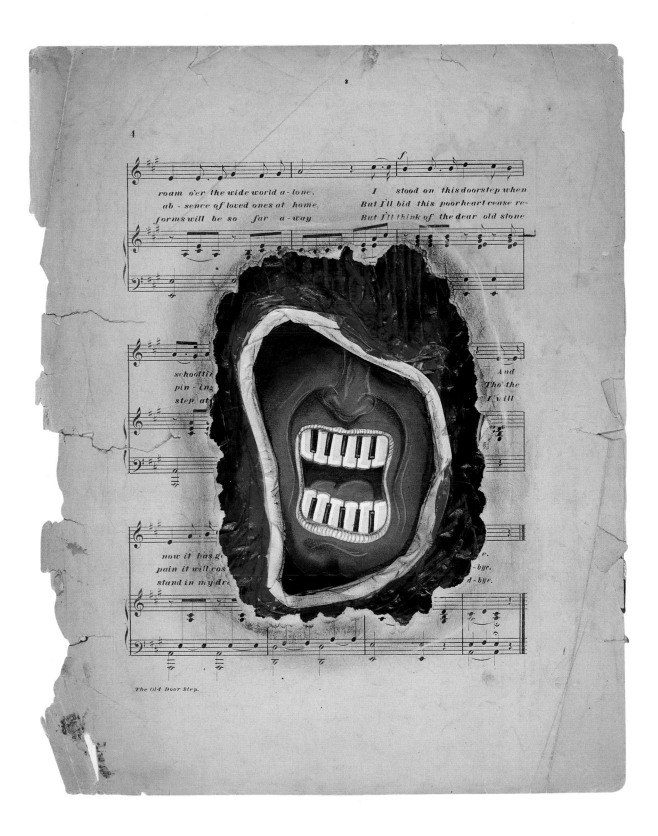

A MAN IN A LOUD SHIRT IS DRIVING ALONG IN HIS CAR AND TURNS ON THE RADIO. HE PROMPTLY HEADS FOR THE NEAREST POLICE STATION AND TURNS HIMSELF IN. WHAT HAPPENED? A MAN IN A LOUD SHIRT IS DRIVING ALONG IN HIS CAR AND TURNS ON THE RADIO. HE PROMPTLY HEADS FOR THE NEAREST POLICE STATION AND TURNS HIMSELF IN. WHAT HAPPENED? A MAN IN A LOUD SHIRT IS DRIVING ALONG IN HIS CAR AND TURNS ON THE RADIO. HE PROMPTLY HEADS FOR THE NEAREST POLICE STATION AND TURNS HIMSELF IN. WHAT HAPPENED? A MAN IN A LOUD SHIRT IS DRIVING ALONG IN HIS CAR AND TURNS ON THE RADIO. HE PROMPTLY HEADS FOR THE NEAREST POLICE STATION AND TURNS HIMSELF IN. WHAT HAPPENED? A MAN IN A LOUD SHIRT IS DRIVING ALONG IN HIS CAR AND TURNS ON THE RADIO. HE PROMPTLY HEADS FOR THE NEAREST POLICE STATION AND TURNS HIMSELF IN. WHAT HAPPENED? A MAN IN A LOUD SHIRT IS DRIVING ALONG IN HIS CAR AND TURNS ON THE RADIO. HE PROMPTLY HEADS FOR THE NEAREST POLICE STATION AND TURNS HIMSELF IN. WHAT HAPPENED? A MAN IN A LOUD SHIRT IS DRIVING ALONG IN HIS CAR AND TURNS ON THE RADIO. HE PROMPTLY HEADS FOR THE NEAREST POLICE STATION AND TURNS HIMSELF IN. WHAT HAPPENED? A MAN IN A LOUD SHIRT IS DRIVING ALONG IN HIS CAR AND TURNS ON THE RADIO. HE PROMPTLY HEADS FOR THE NEAREST POLICE STATION AND TURNS HIMSELF IN. WHAT HAPPENED? A MAN IN A LOUD SHIRT IS DRIVING ALONG IN HIS CAR AND TURNS ON THE RADIO. HE PROMPTLY HEADS FOR THE NEAREST POLICE STATION AND TURNS HIMSELF IN. WHAT HAPPENED? A MAN IN A LOUD SHIRT IS DRIVING ALONG IN HIS CAR AND TURNS ON THE RADIO. HE PROMPTLY HEADS FOR THE NEAREST POLICE STATION AND TURNS HIMSELF IN. WHAT HAPPENED? A MAN IN A LOUD SHIRT IS DRIVING ALONG IN HIS CAR AND TURNS ON THE RADIO. HE PROMPTLY HEADS FOR THE NEAREST POLICE STATION AND TURNS HIMSELF IN. WHAT HAPPENED? A MAN IN A LOUD SHIRT IS DRIVING ALONG IN HIS CAR AND TURNS ON THE RADIO. HE PROMPTLY HEADS FOR THE NEAREST POLICE STATION AND TURNS HIMSELF IN. WHAT HAPPENED? A MAN IN A LOUD SHIRT IS DRIVING ALONG IN HIS CAR AND TURNS ON THE RADIO. HE PROMPTLY HEADS FOR THE NEAREST POLICE STATION AND TURNS HIMSELF IN. WHAT HAPPENED? A MAN IN A LOUD SHIRT IS DRIVING ALONG IN HIS CAR AND TURNS ON THE RADIO. HE PROMPTLY HEADS FOR THE NEAREST POLICE STATION AND TURNS HIMSELF IN. WHAT HAPPENED? A MAN IN A LOUD SHIRT IS DRIVING ALONG IN HIS CAR AND TURNS ON THE RADIO. HE PROMPTLY HEADS FOR THE NEAREST POLICE STATION AND TURNS HIMSELF IN. WHAT HAPPENED? A MAN IN A LOUD SHIRT IS DRIVING ALONG IN HIS CAR AND TURNS ON THE RADIO. HE PROMPTLY HEADS FOR THE NEAREST

A MAN IN A LOUD SHIRT IS DRIVING ALONG IN HIS CAR AND TURNS ON THE RADIO. HE PROMPTLY HEADS FOR THE NEAREST POLICE STATION AND TURNS HIMSELF IN. WHAT HAPPENED?

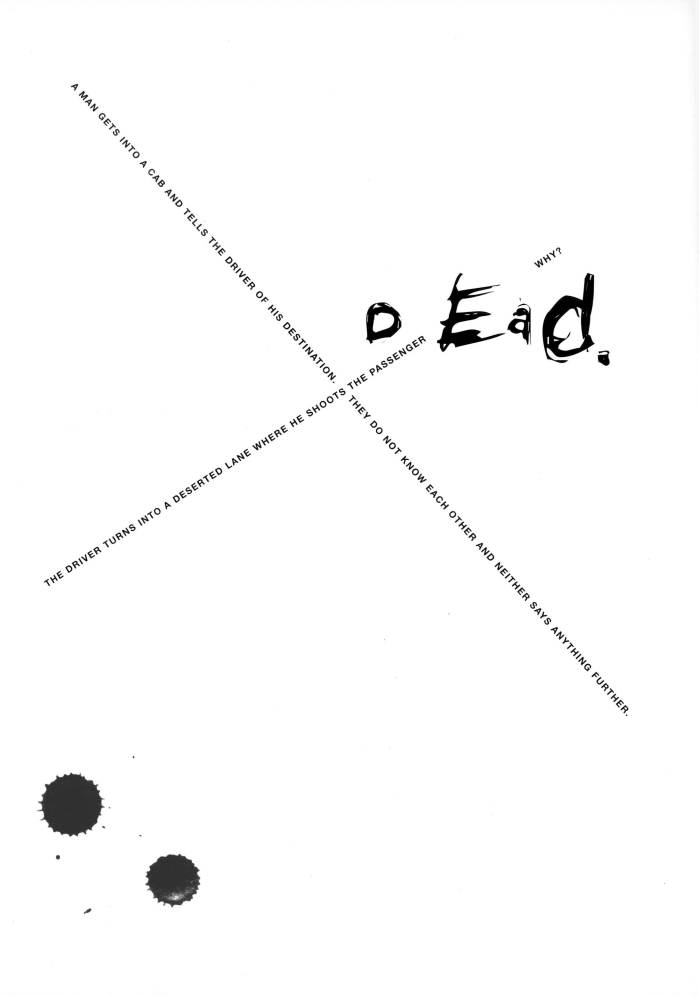

A MAN GETS INTO A CAB AND TELLS THE DRIVER OF HIS DESTINATION.

THE DRIVER TURNS INTO A DESERTED LANE WHERE HE SHOOTS THE PASSENGER

THEY DO NOT KNOW EACH OTHER AND NEITHER SAYS ANYTHING FURTHER.

WHY?

DEaD.

✠

During
World War II
an American
prisoner
of war escaped
from a German
prison camp.
Unfortunately,
he was apprehended
by a particularly
nasty Nazi.
What was it
that gave him
away?

✠

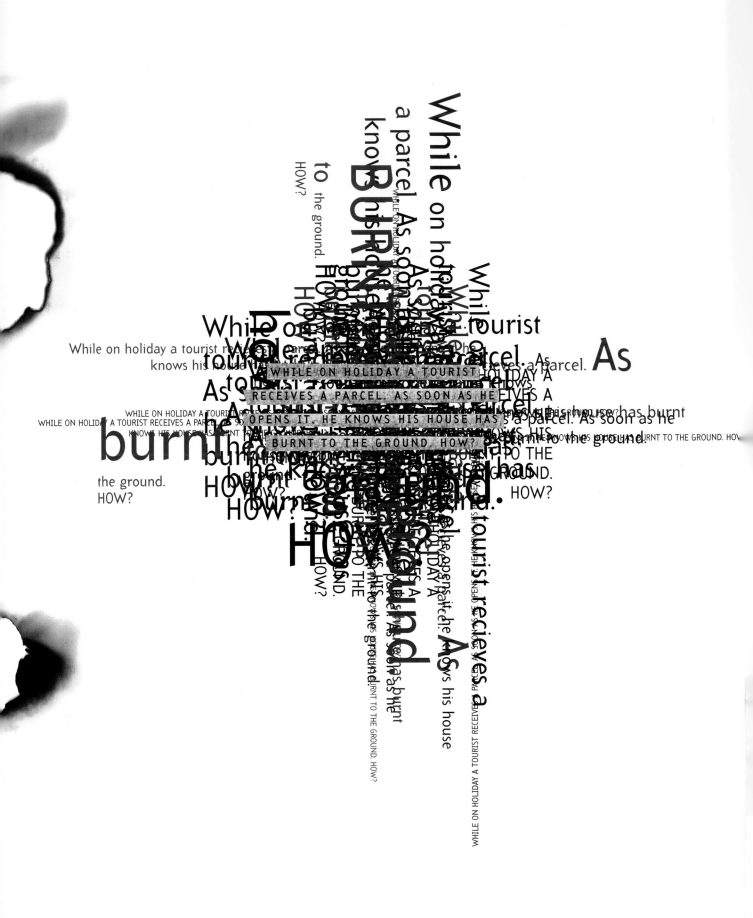

> There once was an animal called the Abbigabby that lived in the mountainous regions of New Zealand. A common problem for the Abbigabby was if it walked past a delicious mountain daisy, it would have to travel the entire way around the mountain to get at it. Why?

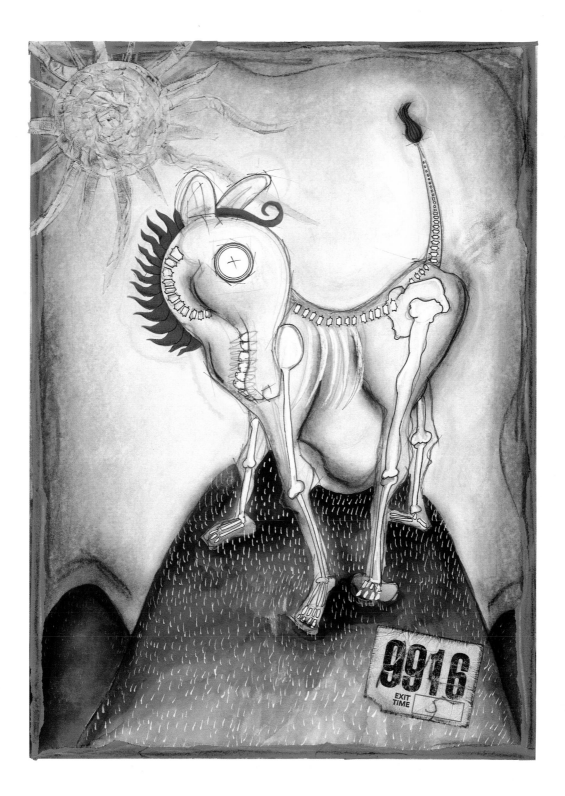

PRIOR TO BECOMING

AN ANGEL, THE WOMAN

HAD FOUND HERSELF

DIVING TOWARD HELL

IN A WET SUIT.

WHAT HAPPENED?

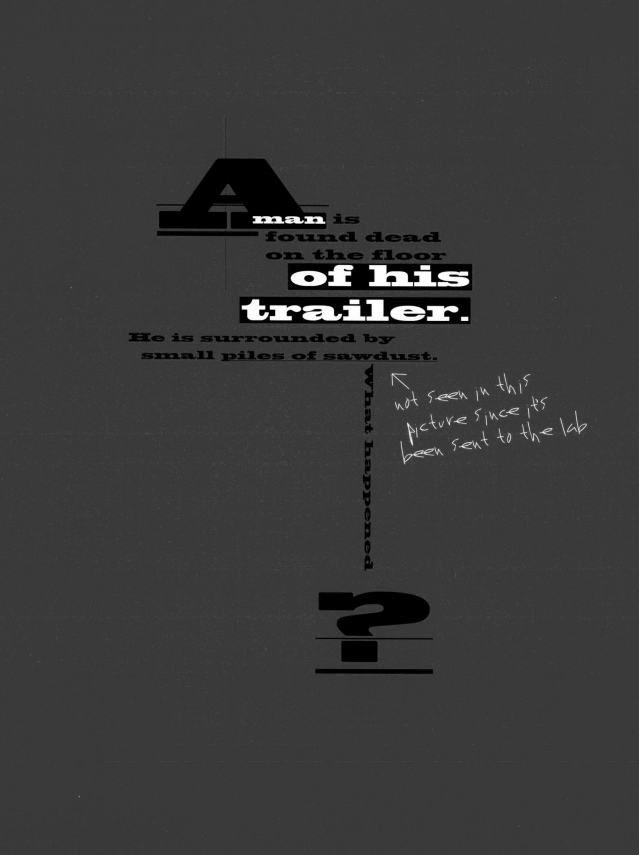

1

 It was a beauty pageant.

2

 He was a lighthouse keeper who got drunk on the job and neglected to turn on the light, which resulted in a ship crashing on the rocks.

3

 The body had no belly button.

4

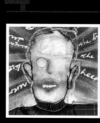 The man was a fisherman. He had been on the phone describing to his wife the size of the fish he'd just caught and put his hands through the phone booth windows.

5

 He was a performing bear in hibernation.

6

 The woman thought she was the last person on earth.

It is an engagement ring.

12

They were at the drive-in movies. She simply drove out.

The man was blind and had ventured outdoors without his trusty seeing-eye dog. (The good news is that the man promptly adopted the boy after kicking him over.)

14

The couple had been rushing to the hospital when the car ran out of gas. She had passed out after giving birth and the stranger was their child.

15

The man had the hiccups.

16

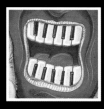

The robed man was a blind-folded tightrope walker who was supposed to step off the rope and onto the platform when the music stopped. The disgruntled understudy who played the organ stopped the music prematurely.

17

The man was a radio disc jockey who had put on a long-playing record; he snuck out of the station, went home, and set fire to his house in order to claim the insurance. On the way back to the station he turned on the radio only to discover the record was stuck and his alibi blown.

18

The cab driver had known for some time that his wife was having an affair. The destination the passenger had given was the driver's own address.

The P.O.W. was an African American.

The man had taken a self-timed photo of himself just before leaving his house to go on vacation. The parcel he received was developed photographs and on close inspection of that particular photograph he could see in the background that he had left the stove on high.

Its two left legs were longer than its two right legs making it impossible for it to turn around without falling down the mountain.

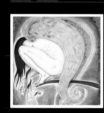

She had been scuba diving in a lake, when a fire department helicopter equipped with a huge water-carrying bucket arrived to scoop up water to douse a forest fire blazing nearby. Unfortunately, she was accidentally scooped up as well.

He was not only the world's smallest man, but he was also blind and slightly crippled. Every night, a jilted lover would sneak into his trailer and saw off a small amount of his walking stick. Thinking he was growing and soon to

MATTHEW JOHNSTONE is currently a senior art director with the advertising agency Foote, Cone & Belding in San Francisco; he held the same position with Saatchi & Saatchi in Sydney, Australia, for three years. A native of New Zealand, Matthew trained as a fine artist, worked as a mural painter, and ran his own theater company before turning to commercial art. He has received several international awards for his work as an art director. He has also lectured in the art of creative thinking.

DR. EDWARD DE BONO is regarded as the leading international authority in both creative thinking and the direct teaching of thinking. Dr. de Bono is the originator of the concept of lateral thinking, which is attributed to him in the *Oxford English Dictionary*. He is the author of more than fifty books, and his work has been translated into more than twenty-five languages. He has made two television series that have been shown around the world. Dr. de Bono's client list includes the top five corporations in the world and such well-known names as Citicorp, Prudential, FedEx, DuPont, NTT (Japan), Ciba-Geigy (Switzerland), and Kuwait Oil Company (Kuwait).

ANNIE SCHWEBEL is a graphic designer currently working in Sydney, Australia.